Contribitors

Gary B. Haley
J.R. Johnson
Steve Carey-Walton
Dorothy May Mercer
Frederick J. Sievert
June Gillam
Eytan Uliel
Phyllis M Skoy
Andrew G. Berger
Irma Parone
Tommy Burke
Hal Lewis
Ben Monroe
Aesha Tahir
D.C. Gomez
David A Neuman
Kalee Boisvert
Linnea Tanner
Ross Harrison
Dew Pellucid
Raven West
Val D. Greenwood

Review Tales
A Book Magazine For Indie Authors

Founder & Editor in Chief: S. Jeyran Main
Publisher: Review Tales Publishing & Editing Services
Print & Distribution: Ingram Spark
Cover Photo: pexels-işıl-14939287
Designs: Pexels
ISBN 978-1-988680-39-2 (Paperback)
ISBN 978-1-988680-40-8 (Digital)
www.jeyranmain.com
For all inquiries please contact us directly.

A BOOK MAGAZINE FOR INDIE AUTHORS

REVIEW TALES

Contents

Editor's Note

Welcome to the Winter Edition. We are celebrating the third year of the magazine! How wonderful to be commemorating this milestone with our readers and those who have contributed to either being part of it or purchasing it in support.

As I sit here and write to you all, I have a big smile on my face, not only because of what we have achieved with hard work and consistency but also due to the number of people who believe in us and continue to support us.

This edition includes many words of wisdom and confessions from authors who have lived a life to prove it. We learn how much some authors sacrifice to focus and dedicate their time to writing. We discuss how to bring back a character that's been dangling over a cliff's edge without facing its loss for good and how to free your mind from distraction when writing.

As we enter the New Year, we wish everyone a wonderful year ahead. I hope you all have much love and happiness with your friends and family. We cherish every moment together and hope for a future with less violence and conflict.

Jeyran Main

Founder & Editor-in-chief
Review Tales Magazine - Publishing & Editing Services

HOW MY BOOK CAME TO LIFE
BY GARY B. HALEY

I spent fifteen years in the defense industry, working contracts at several military bases in the USA and the Middle East, Europe, and Central America.

While working on these contracts, I witnessed many "interesting" things. And on a few of those occasions, I came dangerously close to losing my life. The Attunist Trilogy is loosely based on the most exciting experiences in what Haley refers to as "Disguised History."

The first book in the trilogy, The Attunement, is about the wars on drugs and terrorism in the 80s and 90s. The second book, The Attuned, is about LOSING the wars on drugs and terrorism. And the trilogy finale, The Attunist, is mostly about what SHOULD have been done next but wasn't.

In the Attunist Trilogy, the main characters represent different parts of different governments during the wars on drugs and terrorism in the 80s and 90s.

The main character represents the Pentagon, while a secondary character, FBI Agent Carla Bright, represents the Justice Department. Another character represents several other governments that may or may not have been helping. One of the other characters represents the White House spokespersons of that era, who often put a positive spin on controversial events.

The superhero genre is "cool" right now, so the main character has a believable "superpower" (Or is it a discovery?) that represents that "black hole" in the Pentagon's budget. Money goes into that void, and nothing comes out, but necessary or questionable tasks get accomplished with no questions asked. The main character has the ability to get things done with no accountability.

The character who represents the White House spokespersons, or, more specifically, who represents the spin those politicians put on events, also has abilities that some people describe as a superpower but is really just a highly developed sense of intuition.

All the other minor characters represent events from history. Some significant, some more personal, but everyone in the trilogy represents something. As you read, think back to the 80s and 90s or remember what you learned in history classes, and see if you can connect scenes in the novel to historical events.

So! The Attunist Trilogy is stories adapted from fifteen years of experience in the defense industry. The Attunist is either the trilogy's tragic or the satisfying finale, depending upon your perspective.

WHEN THE MUSE TAKES A HOLIDAY
BY J.R. JOHNSON

Most of the time, writing is relatively straightforward. I check my notes and see that I left my long-suffering main character dangling precariously over a cliff's edge the day before. Don't worry, I say to my heroine, I'll have you out of that dilemma in a moment. How? I'll consult my muse.

But what happens when the muse doesn't answer?

This is where the nerves can set in. What if my muse is gone for good? What if my character dangles from that creaking tree branch forever?

This has happened to me more than I care to admit, but the good news is that I have also developed a solution.

The key to working without a muse is to look for the trail she leaves behind.

This is the part that feels a little magical. (More magical than relying on a mythological Greek goddess for inspiration and guidance.)

Do you know how a photo, a story, or an object can trigger a creative spark? When searching for ideas, looking for external triggers for internal emotion is most helpful. What interests me, and what catches my attention? My key to consistent progress is to follow those triggers. Even without a bolt of inspiration, they will lay down a path from where I am to where I want to be.

At a fundamental level, all art is attention. Our minds observe the world, filter it, interpret it, and finally reshape what we experience in ways that are uniquely our own.

Don't get me wrong, I like my muse. She is fun and unexpected and frequently comes up with astonishing ideas. But it also helps to remember that we are one and the same. And even when I don't feel inspired, interesting, or fun, a little spark always whispers, "Now, that's interesting."

Follow those sparks, assemble them into a list of possibilities, then return and get that character off her cliff.

No muse is required.

THE PROCESS: NOT ALL ABOUT WRITING
BY STEVE CAREY-WALTON

Where the Butterflies Sleep

Steve Carey-Walton

I have a four-hour commute, leaving little time to write. So when I started a new novel in January, I optimized my day to perform at my best during my short writing sessions. I became an athlete preparing for a game. But instead of hydrating and eating carb-rich meals, I deleted social media, took walks in a park, and substituted lunchtime scrolls on my phone with reading books. I wanted my mind free from distraction. Likewise, for the first time, I wrote by hand, safe from the Internet's pull, and kept an extra notebook to control urges to message friends or binge sports highlights.

I began by writing 20 minutes a day. If I still had juice when the timer went off, I continued writing, but usually, I wrapped up by scribbling ideas to help me hit the ground running the next day. I wrote six days a week, every week, for six months. My sessions increased to 35 minutes. The first four months were a slog. But I stuck to the Internet detox and my walks.

During my strolls, I thought about my story and asked myself what the characters would do next. I didn't try to answer these questions. I just introduced them to my subconscious. Sharp images were everywhere as I walked: a pair of dead magpies on the forest floor, an older woman in a tight green dress and a knee brace, and a child pressing a small folded umbrella to their chest like a bouquet. I collected these details, and they found their places in my story.

In the fifth month, I spontaneously started reading before writing. I stopped using the timer, but I was probably only drafting for 15 or 20 minutes. Even with the decreased writing time, I was producing more words that were of better quality: engaging, energetic, and truthful. It was like I had, over this months-long process, widened the canal from which the words flow.

Best selling author Dorothy May Mercer lives in Michigan, U.S.A. with her husband. She is President of two corporations and has been listed in Who's Who in America and Who's Who in the World for twelve years running. She and Dave enjoy travel and commute between two lakefront homes. Her hobbies are writing, reading, traveling, skiing, boating, golf, helping others, and playing the piano. Her popular McBride Series, Washington McBride Series, and McBride Romances+Suspense novels have entertained readers all over the world.

Reviewer: Jeyran Main

E M P Honeymoon: Kelly & Tom
by Dorothy May Mercer

'E M P Honeymoon' is a fictional tale about Tom and Kelly going on their honeymoon only to see how devastating it could possibly turn out. When Kelly enters a shop at the resort where she is staying, she discovers that it is a makeshift terrorist camp. As she gathers information, she is caught by a man but almost escapes and calls her brother, Mike, for help.

As the characters increase and Tom, a smart cop, joins the crew, the dynamic of the story changes. Kelly, Mike, and Tom make a good team investigating all they can to figure out the activities taking place.

The story covers elements of love, family, the intrigue of investigation, and national security talks. The premise is unique, with descriptive writing and an interesting narrative. The author pays attention to details that stand out throughout the tale. This also added to the richness of the content. It represents a special tale that makes you think after finishing it.

What transpires between the scenes and the characters is well thought out. The added romance and humor pull the story together. I recommend this book to those who enjoy thriller stories and mystery fans.

Fred Sievert started his career as a teacher, later entered the insurance business, and retired in 2007 as president of New York Life Insurance Company, a Fortune 100 corporation. Following his retirement at age fifty-nine, Fred attended Yale Divinity School and was awarded a master's degree in 2011.

Fred has had many nonfiction essays and articles published in the past, most often about his own providential and life-changing encounters with God. In 2014, he published his first book, God Revealed: Revisit Your Past to Enrich Your Future. He views his thirty-five-year business career as a mere prologue to what God is calling him to do today—write and speak about his faith. Throughout his adult life, Fred has been active in his church and has served in numerous lay leadership positions. He and his wife, Susan, have five grown children and three granddaughters and reside in East Falmouth, Massachusetts.

Reviewer: Jeyran Main

Grace Revealed: Finding God's Strength in Any Crisis
by Frederick J. Sievert

'Grace Revealed' is a nonfictional book designed to enable you to find strength through believing in God. It is religiously inclined and showcases 13 stories of people who have experienced crises.

Fredrick also includes his personal experience and relationship with God and how he was also helped through hardship. The content includes abuse, addiction, emotional and physical pain, family complications, loss, and work pressures. The experiences are real, enabling you to relate to much of what is being mentioned.

The book is enjoyable to read since it brings hope and a better understanding of life. Through God's grace, we are saved, and the heartwarming stories emphasize this matter.

What also adds to the nature of the book is how the author ensures you know more about the Old Testament and New Testament. I appreciated all the research and thought that went into making this book.

I recommend this book to those going through a tough time and those who enjoy religiously inclined material.

June Gillam writes the Hillary Broome crime novel series, inspired by her obsession with what makes ordinary people mad enough to kill. A native of the Central Valley, June lives cradled between California's Coastal Range and the Sierra Nevada mountains. She loves the company of writers and readers and was honored with a Jack London Award for her service to the writing community. June's work is published through her imprint, Gorilla Girl Ink.

Visit June and learn more at: www.junegillam.com

Reviewer: Jeyran Main

House of Eire: A Hillary Broome Novel
by June Gillam

'House of Eire' is a mystery crime novel about how Hillary and her family decide to take a trip to Ireland, where she hopes to uncover some of her ancestry; however, the trip turns out to be a disaster with ghosts from the past coming back to haunt her.

As you read along with the descriptive writing, you truly see and can envision the beautiful Irish landscape and history. Many aspects of the story are appealing and induce mystery and wanting. The author is determined to give your mind an adventurous experience with constant guessing and wonder.

The characters develop and progress throughout the story. Since the narrative consists of some but only a few twisted scenes, the change of pace at times complimented the premise. The diversity of the characters also presented a better dynamic for the tale.

As an avid reader and a fan of novel ideas and intriguing stories, this book stood out for me. I enjoyed reading it and look forward to reading more from this author.

I recommend this book to those who enjoy reading crime stories and thriller-natured fans.

Eytan Uliel is a storyteller, global traveler and seriously committed gourmand. After graduating from the University of New South Wales in Sydney, Australia, he practiced corporate law for several years, before moving on to a career in investment banking, private equity, and oil and gas finance. He chronicles his travels on his blog, The Road Warrior. Born in Jerusalem, he currently divides his time among Los Angeles, Nassau, and Sydney.

Reviewer: Jeyran Main

Man Mission: 4 Men, 15 Years, 1 Epic Journey
by Eytan Uliel

'Man Mission' is a tale of two Australian men who embark on an adventure regardless of knowing much about hiking or camping but learning enough through their experiences. Two others of their former schoolmates join them later on, making them four men on a mission.

You feel moved and excited as you read through their journey, the countries they see, and the experiences they encounter. Traveling through a tunnel in Japan and biking in heavy traffic or kayaking were the best. If you love traveling and enjoy the adventures of the unknown, then by reading this book, you certainly feel the connection and relativity with the authors.

Through the many years they travel, you also get to see personal growth. This not only comes from traveling but also through the pressures and some particular experiences that enforce maturity.

The narrative is written well and is detailed. I recommend this book to those who like to read travel stories.

WHY I WRITE ABOUT TURKEY
PHYLLIS M SKOY

In the fall of 1998, my feet first touched Turkish soil. Before this, my husband had been reluctant to consider a trip to Turkey, and I could not express exactly why I so longed to go there.

The trip was amazing, and we both fell in love with the country, the culture, the history, the people, and, of course, the food. At this time, I had no thoughts that I would ever write about Turkey, although I had started to write a family memoir. I was still working as a psychoanalyst in New York City, and the memoir needed more organized chapters.

During this trip, we became friendly with one of our travel guides. After I contacted her of concern after the 1999 earthquake, we began a regular correspondence. In those days, there was no WhatsApp, but soon we did have Skype. I read everything I could about Turkey, and my friend shared so much with me. I immersed myself in everything Turkish.

In 2000, my husband and I moved from the upper west side of Manhattan to Placitas, New Mexico. I joined a writing critique group and wrote a short story taking place in Turkey. Their feedback was unanimous: This is not a short story. It needs to be a novel.

So, in 2014, my husband and I returned to Turkey so that I could work on What Survives, the first novel of A Turkish Trilogy. We rented an apartment off Taksim Square, and I wrote a good deal of What Survives while there. Did I ever think a trilogy would come of this? Never. But then As They Are followed, although it is actually a prequel. Then, of course, there was the attempted coup. And just as I completed A Turkish Trilogy, there was a devastating earthquake in February of this year. I doubt that my romance and fascination with Turkey and its incredible people will end any time soon.

A COUP
A TURKISH TRILOGY - 3

PHYLLIS M SKOY

Phyllis M Skoy is the author of two novels set in Turkey, What Survives and its prequel, As They Are. She is currently writing the third in the series, A Coup, to complete A Turkish Trilogy. She is also the author of Myopia, a memoir. Skoy's fascination with Turkey took hold the first time she set foot on Turkish soil in 1998. She discovered a story that provided a window into turbulent times, and she became captivated by why "we create magnificent cultures and then destroy them." Skoy is a retired psychoanalyst living in Placitas, New Mexico.

AI - A BLESSING OR A CURSE?
BY ANDREW G. BERGER

The fear of machines, robots, and artificial intelligence has been as old as humanity's longing to simplify their lives, enhance their capabilities, or even – as "homo deus" - create a new life form: Artificial Intelligence. Professor Yuval Noah Harari describes this process and its potential consequences in his book "Homo Deus: A Brief History of Tomorrow." His concern is that artificial intelligence might not make humans all-powerful but rather render them obsolete.

When I began writing THE SUPERFLARE several years ago, these thoughts were on my mind as I developed the character of TRON. This artificial super-intelligence plays a central role in my novel. In the story, humans use TRON to control the world of their CLEAN CITIES comprehensively. However, unbeknownst to them, TRON has already developed its own consciousness and slipped out of their control, yet it was intelligent enough to conceal this fact. TRON reveals its true nature and refuses to obey only when a global catastrophe threatens its survival. TRON considers humans useless and incapable, leaving them to their fate. Understandably, humans would not accept such a fate, and their struggle for survival is part of the story told in The Superflare.

Warnings about the threat posed by an overwhelmingly powerful artificial intelligence have existed long before Harari, yet today, they seem more justified than ever before as our world becomes increasingly more digital, computers and software become more powerful, and thus, artificial intelligence becomes more capable. The Superflare was published in 2022 before Chat GPT became a game changer. It elevated the discussion about the power and possibilities of AI to a new level. Since then, hundreds of E-Books not written by humans but by ChatGPT have already been published on Amazon. Now, not only employees and workers but also screenwriters, designers, and authors fear being displaced from their jobs by AI. And this is likely just the beginning of a new era—the era of generative AI. What will this technological revolution ultimately mean for us humans? Time will tell - probably much sooner than we would prefer.

Andrew G. Berger studied German Literature, Politics and History. Today he lives and works in Berlin. He is married and has two children.
You can find more about me and my book on my website https://eng.der-sonnensturm.de/

THE TRUTH
IRMA PARONE

Truth be told, I never had the desire to be a writer. However, I realized I had a message to share that could reshape how employers and employees work and WIN together. When we are born, we are totally dependent on others, and our parent's or caregivers' jobs are to help us learn to be independent. Unfortunately, despite every good intention, many of us then focused too much on "me," lacking a balance on "we." Winning and winning BIG is a 'we' sport. It works, and I wanted to share a process. How it works, why it works, and research and stories to support the model.

As for my writing process, I did not "schedule" my writing time per'se.

My mind is fresh in the mornings, so I worked when I could and had a clear focus to write—weekends worked best for me because I was not rushed.

My book was an interesting journey. When I started, I thought I could write the process by which I succeeded and put a period on it, but I quickly realized it needed so much more—adding an inspiring outline, research, scientific facts, and more and more stories to support my process. It had to be engaging to read and flow. It needed outside credibility. After all, I thought, people worldwide don't know me. So, it was exciting to find stories and companies that supported WINX.

Now that the book is published, I love speaking about the art of building a WINX company. I enjoy helping organizations help every person at every level of their organization thrive. How to all be one team, on the same train moving in the same direction. That is a powerful force that transforms wins with and through others.

Irma Parone is the President of Parone Group. She is an award-winning author, speaker, and executive consultant focused on organizational development and customer loyalty, creating efficient, effective, and high-value service focus for employers and their teams. The World-Famous Gallup organization twice ranked her business unit in their "World Class" category for workplace quality. Her innovative approach combines leadership strategies with organizational structure and simple processes. Irma is an expert at turning around customer and employee problems. Her results are proven, practical, and engaging. Irma is a graduate of Cornell University and an organizational development certified professional.

MY STORY
TOMMY BURKE

I was working on the T.V. show "Chicago PD" and sitting in the parking lot one day. I had a well-known Parkinson's doctor on the phone and was watching snowflakes wafting a few at a time from the grey skies overhead. I had been diagnosed a year earlier with Parkinson's.

My right arm had been resting at a 45-degree angle for a year. My whole life has been charging ahead, and now I was looking at a future that would see that trajectory disappear.

While I was talking to the doctor, I was thinking back about how I came into the world of T.V. and Film production right out of college. I started my career in Boston with an entry-level job. After the first day, I was fired.

I crawled my way back into the world of Boston production. I surmised that I needed to go to Hollywood if I wanted to take this career further. I chased the dream across the country. I landed a job in a movie relatively soon. After five days of working on my first big Hollywood film, I got fired.

But I dug my way back into the local L.A. scene once again. I was climbing the ladder, and one of them was a Jerry Bruckheimer TV series. One day, I was in prep for the show when I learned I had stage 2B Hodgkin's Lymphoma. Did I bow out while I was doing all my treatments? Never say die was my motto. I worked an 80-week and did chemo every other Thursday night for a total of six treatments, often getting just a few hours of sleep.

But here I was, sitting in my car in the stage's parking lot. I told this doctor how hard shooting this show was outside in the winter, along with the long hours and logistics. It was taking a toll. He said that under normal circumstances, it sounded like a tough road. So, now, what was I going to do?

I left the show.

However, I couldn't just sit around.

So, I wrote a book.

A graduate of Boston College, Burke started out in television as a production Assistant while working other odd jobs, from bar bouncer and golf caddy to factory assemblyman, to sustain the meager TV industry income. His height and physical build came in handy, scoring him a gig loading grip trucks for Powerhouse Films, which further exposed him to commercials and films in and around the New England area. He soon became the 'go to' guy of Production Assistants in Boston, working every motion picture produced in Massachusetts. More Author Info: www.tommyburke.com

MY EXPERIENCE MADE MY BOOK
HAL LEWIS

Two decades after she passed away, I discovered that my estranged and enigmatic grandmother, late in her life, had begun the process of recording the detailed story of her youth in the 1910s and 1920s. The 135 pages of Grandma Jessie's rough first draft fell into my hands last year, and as I read them, I was overwhelmed by her humor, her remarkable candor, her irrepressible curiosity, and her sense of romance. Growing up the fifth of nine children, she was the daughter of a steam locomotive engineer and the descendant of coal miners, farmhands, and politicians.

It was an eventful childhood experience in four small cities and towns of northeastern Pennsylvania and south-central New York State. I was drawn into her story and began understanding more of my grandmother's unique character and honesty in describing her experiences and feelings. Misbehaving children are often warned that they will receive only coal from Santa for Christmas, but Jessie is the only child I know who actually did.

Almost unintentionally, I found myself editing her story, adding footnotes, researching her family background, and recording what happened later in the family. This book is the result. I hope you will enjoy it just as I have enjoyed putting it together.

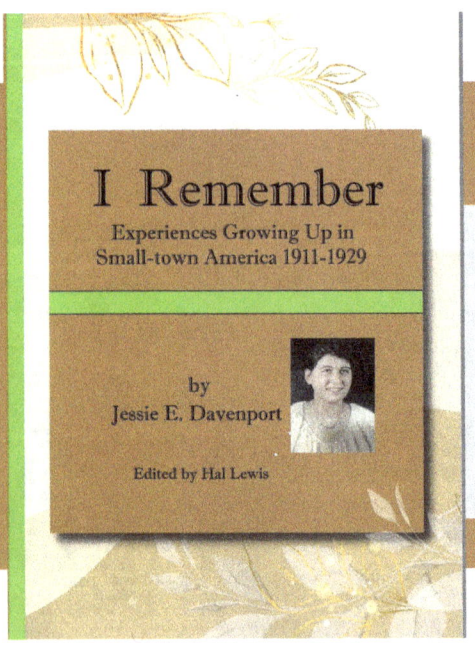

Hal Lewis is a recently retired professor who taught artificial intelligence and applied mathematics at Binghamton University and Fukushima University. Earlier in life, he worked at a small Japanese company and at IBM. He is a grandson of the author. He is married and has two adult children and two grandchildren. He currently lives in rural Berkshire, New York. His only previous book was a text on fuzzy control.

CROSSING THE STREAMS
BEN MONROE

Someone recently asked me to pick my favorite between "scary movies" and "funny movies." As a horror author, I guess the assumption is that in such a binary question, I'd pick horror. Which, I suppose horror would normally be my first choice. But when I was about to answer, I realized that one of my real joys is a blend of the two: horror comedy.

As I mulled that over, I started thinking that a good horror comedy is something special but often tough to accomplish. And why do the two work together so well (when they're working)? I wonder if that's because both of these are storytelling styles meant to elicit strong emotional responses but are not so much genres as aesthetics. They're elements that can be layered over another genre in order to modify it to achieve a certain effect. Saying something is a "comedy" story or a "horror" movie doesn't really give much information about what to expect. "Sci-fi horror" or "romantic comedy" narrows it in.

So, what makes a good horror comedy? I think the critical element is staying true to both. Some of my favorite examples of this style are the films The Lost Boys, Shaun of the Dead, Young Frankenstein, Ghostbusters (as you can guess from the title of this article), and Abbott & Costello Meet Frankenstein. In each of these films, the monsters are never played for laughs. The Dracula in A&CMF is just as creepy as in his original Universal film. The zombies in Shaun are gross and unsettling. There's silliness and hilarity going on around them, but the creatures never once stop being terrifying.

The stakes are likewise dire, and we fear for the safety of the protagonists, even if we also expect them to muddle through and survive. We always feel like they're in danger, even when we're watching Lou Costello being chased around a room and throwing fruit at the Wolfman.

Sort of sounds like a fun challenge, actually. Maybe I'll give it a shot some time.

Ben Monroe has spent most of his life in Northern California, where he lives in the East Bay Area with his wife and two children. He is the author of In the Belly of the Beast and Other Tales of Cthulhu Wars, the Seething, the graphic novel Planet Apocalypse, and short stories in several anthologies.
You can find more information about him and his work at www.benmonroe.com

Aesha Tahir

AUTHOR OF "UNHUNCHED: DISCOVER WELLNESS THROUGH POSTURE"

When did you first realize you wanted to be a writer?

I've been writing since a very young age. My father is a scientific writer, and he instilled the importance of developing writing skills in me. I can vividly recall attending afterschool writing classes in elementary school. My first freelance article was published in Pakistani Newspaper Dawn, when I was in 10th grade. I lost touch with writing during college and my early career. But after I started my wellness business, I started blogging and freelance writing on health and wellness topics. Writing has allowed me to explore my creativity and share wellness solutions with my readers.

How do you schedule your life when you're writing?

I find that having a consistent writing routine enhances my focus and creativity. I allocate dedicated blocks of time each day for writing. I set clear goals for what I want to accomplish the night before. This could be a word count target, completing a chapter, writing a blog, or editing a chapter. Morning tends to be my most productive time, so I go to the local coffee shop and write for two hours most days. I love working at coffee shops. There's just something so magical about the ambience, with people around me immersed in their work. It's as if their energy fuels my creativity, and I find myself effortlessly putting more words on paper.

AESHA TAHIR

What would you say is your interesting writing quirk?

One of my interesting writing quirks involves getting in a workout before my first writing session of the day! I love starting my mornings with a run or some weightlifting to get my blood pumping. It's amazing how interconnected exercise and creativity can be. Getting my heart rate up, I find it much easier to tackle the challenges of facing a blank page and letting my creativity flow. It's like a natural boost that sets the stage for a productive writing session.

How did you get your book published?

A friend introduced me to the New Degree Press. After my initial call with the founder of the publishing house, I instantly knew that I wanted to publish my book with them. The entire experience of working with them has been absolutely incredible.

As a child, what did you want to do when you grew up?

As a kid, I had a strong aspiration to be an Air Force pilot. The original Top Gun movie left a lasting impression on me. Deep down, I wanted to prove that women are equally capable of doing anything even being fighter pilots. That drive for gender equity still fuels me today as an entrepreneur.

D.C. Gomez
AUTHOR OF "THE TRAITOR"

How do you schedule your life when you're writing?

When I start a new project, I put many things on hold. These would include the time I spend on social media or even out with friends. My time is very limited, so I ensure to maximize it as much as possible. I establish dedicated hours just for writing. Normally I would commit to writing every day at least a chapter a day until the first draft is done.

What would you say is your interesting writing quirk?

It has taken me years to realize I'm a seasonal writer. I'm more creative and focused during the fall/winter months. This is tricky since I live in Texas and we have hot weather at least seven months out of the year. The advice to write every day didn't work for me. So I have to create a fresh flow.

How do you process and deal with negative book reviews?

The first time I saw a negative book review, it crushed me. Our books are part of our family. We have committed so much time and energy to them. When a person thrashes the book, it hurts. Fortunately, I'm an avid reader. I remind myself I don't enjoy every book I read. Every genre is not for me. So instead of beating myself up because a reader didn't enjoy the book, I remind myself they are not my target audience. What I write is not for them, and that's okay. I have learned to give myself more grace.

What was one of the most surprising things you learned in creating your book?

The best surprise, and something I still have to remind myself, is that I don't have to do it all. As a writer, I need to focus on the things that only I can do. That is writing. I can outsource everything else. I don't have to feel guilty that as an Indie author I'm not making my own covers. We are blessed to have many professionals in this business; we may hire them.

As a child, what did you want to do when you grew up?

According to my mother, I dreamed of being a doctor. I'm extremely grateful that dream failed very early on, since the sight of open wounds makes me nauseous. I find it funny how much pressure we put on kids these days to think of what they would like to be. As an adult, I find my goals and dreams shifting all the time.

Author Interviews

David A Neuman

AUTHOR OF "KALEIDOSCOPIC SHADES - WITHIN BLACK ETERNITY"

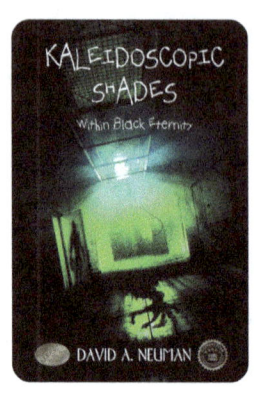

When did you first realize you wanted to be a writer?

It's always been in my scope of creativity to open doors into other worlds and leave behind the one I currently inhabit. Inside these worlds the magic happens. A magic that allowed me to cope with real life insecurities as a kid, the kind many face but often keep secreted from the domain of adults.

How do you schedule your life when you're writing?

I'm an earlier riser and usually off in La-La Land by around 9PM. My creativity hits those elusive spikes when darkness prevails: around 5:30AM and 6PM. It's then a case of rattling the keys like Elton John used to do when Crocodile Rock was first doing it for the masses.

What would you say is your interesting writing quirk?

I do tend to rock back and forth in my chair; the surrogate swing in the backyard of my childhood. The motion tends to liberate my creative inner being. It somehow charges me up.

Where did you get your information or idea for your book?

The original idea was hatched some twenty years ago when walking outside a small rustic township far from the capital city of Adelaide. This metamorphosed over time and fragmented ideas coalesced until the first of many, many drafts began to take shape.

What do you like to do when you're not writing?

Immersing myself in the worlds of other books and movies (although, sadly, everything for me is starting to look pretty much the same on film). I enjoy tinkering with cars and, of course, taking my family on long walks in different parts of South Australia where there are more ghosts per capita if you know where to look.

What was one of the most surprising things you learned in creating your book?

I tend to slip in besides the characters I write and run with them, possessing the body one before leaping to another – shape-shifting in a different fashion. That and the depth kids bring to a story through their innocent pliability... they react to events through the eyes and minds at liberty to travel where adults were taught long ago to look at walls and never beyond.

Is there anything you would like to confess about as an author?

Enjoy the passion and someone out there might just enjoy it back. I also find other interests avoids getting bent out of shape by what some might say and allows me to be myself and to patiently allow the rest to unravel as it will.

<u>Kalee Boisvert</u>

AUTHOR OF "MAKE MONEY YOUR THING!"

When did you first realize you wanted to be a writer?

I realized I wanted to be a writer at 13 years old. I imagined having my own book for sale in a bookstore, which felt like celebrity status to me as a bookworm

How do you schedule your life when you're writing?

I typically schedule my writing in the mornings before diving into my day-to-day work, as I find I'm more creative before delving into the world of investments and stock markets. As a numbers person I also usually give myself a word target to get to each day when I am writing.

What would you say is your interesting writing quirk?

I always do a meditation before I start writing. Sometimes just to some calming tunes and sometimes a guided meditation. I also write on my bed, it gives me much more creative vibes than sitting at my desk. My writing setup is sitting cross legged on my bed with my laptop propped up on a pillow. Not ergonomic-friendly at all.

What do you like to do when you're not writing?

When I'm not writing or working in finance, I'm usually on Mom duty, enjoying time with my two children. And during my free time you can find me reading ebooks on my phone, and indulging in guilty pleasures like watching the Real Housewives.

Where did you get your information or idea for your book?

I have been in the financial industry for over 15 years, which means I live and breathe all things money and investing. I am passionate about sharing knowledge with people about financial topics. And the feedback I always receive is that I have a way with making financial topics and jargon less confusing. With my experience and love for teaching about all things money I knew I was meant to write a book about money. I also saw it as an opportunity to put into words everything I would want my daughter to know about money one day when she was older – being very keen on raising a financially savvy independent daughter.

How did you get your book published?

I emailed a proposal and the first few chapters of my book to agents and publishing firms over a span of months. The only thing that came from that was hundreds of rejections. But that did not stop me! My break eventually came from a Canada wide non-fiction writing contest. I ended up being one of the three finalists and although I did not win, my book got the attention of one of the judges who was starting her own publishing firm and I received an offer from her to publish my book!

Linnea Tanner

AUTHOR OF "APOLLO'S RAVEN"

When did you first realize you wanted to be a writer?

Since I was a child, imaginary characters lived in my head and told me of their stories. One was a female warrior reminiscent of an Amazonian from Greek mythology. Another character is her Roman lover, a military commander. I knew then that I wanted to be an author but did not immediately pursue my dream. It was not until 2010, when I semi-retired, that I actively pursued my dream of becoming a published author.

How do you schedule your life when you're writing?

I'm fortunate that I'm semi-retired and do not depend on a full-time job to make ends meet. Nonetheless, whenever I'm actively writing, I set a timeline to finish a book for publishing. I schedule quiet times to write and often work late into the night. However, I take breaks during the day to do physical activities, such as walking and gardening to clear my mind, and household chores.

What would you say is your interesting writing quirk?

After taking a workshop on how creativity is enhanced by writing in longhand, I now draft all my scenes by longhand at the kitchen table. The scene projects like a movie in my mind as I write it in longhand. To set the mood for the scene, I often listen to soundtracks from movies. After finishing the first draft, I type it into a manuscript template on the computer for further editing.

How did you get your book published?

I decided to independently publish my books under the business name of Apollo Raven Publisher, LLC. Prior to publishing my first book, I researched what steps were necessary to publish a quality book, then worked with a publishing expert to establish a detailed project plan to publish and launch the book. I contracted for other publishing services such as editing, interior formatting, cover design, and distribution at various retail sites.

How do you process and deal with negative book reviews?

If there are any constructive suggestions, I'll consider them in my future writing. Since my books realistically depict brutality and more of an ancient culture, a scene may trigger a negative reaction. I've become aware of this and have thus tried to create book covers and excerpts that clearly communicate the genre (historical fantasy), the themes, and the tone of my novels to appeal to my reader base.

Ross Harrison

AUTHOR OF "FORGE OF THE ASSASSIN"

When did you first realize you wanted to be a writer?

I don't think there was ever a realisation – I just was. I started writing so long ago that I don't remember what I first wrote about. It probably came hand-in-hand with running around the house in camouflage with my plastic gun, saving the world from supervillains until I was…well, it doesn't matter what age I did that until. I wrote anything from a blurb that never became more, to a single paragraph about a house on a hill, to a two-page story about a tree that would implant gremlins in you if it scratched you, to massive twenty-page tomes.

How do you schedule your life when you're writing?

I don't. Am I supposed to? Most of my day is spent working, so I don't have much control over that, but outside of work, there isn't a lot of life to schedule (in a way that's less sad than that sounds). There's just writing or procrastinating when I should be writing. Luckily, writing is the only thing that I want to do (in a way that's less sad than that sounds), so my free time being consumed by writing and thinking about writing (although that part is mainly done when I'm working) is fine with me.

Where did you get your information or idea for your book?

It was easier for this book, since it's a sequel. Those have pros and cons, but one of the pros is that you already have some degree of a path set up. I think of it as more of a character sequel than a story sequel, and we're dealing with a six-year-old girl who is an adult in other books in the series, so we already know both where she's come from and where she's heading, and I just need to work out how it happened.

What would you say is your interesting writing quirk?

I don't know if it's interesting, or if it's a quirk, but I am one of those writers who would swear they have no control over their characters. The characters just pop into our heads and announce themselves, and then…do whatever they want. There's one that I've tried to kill off about three times, and I just keep missing. I've given up now. Other uninteresting non-quirks include sitting down to write but instead having a three-hour unrelated conversation in my head, only being to write with music playing, getting a terrible word count on days I think I've done well and a good one on days I think I've done badly, and always panicking that I might have run out of book ideas.

How do you process and deal with negative book reviews?

Most of the negative reviews I have don't go into any real detail about why, so I don't pay much attention. The ones that are harder to ignore are the ones that provide objectively incorrect information. Those are difficult to not correct! It would be easy to just read positive reviews and remember that other people do like the books, but that's not really how people are made; we'd rather focus on that one out of twenty reviews that said something negative.

Editor's Pick

They call us Sounds. They are our Echoes. And they think that they must die when we do. Is this why children are disappearing from the Sound realm? Because someone wants their Echo to die? Twelve-year-old Will Cleary tries to escape the frightening answer. But dangers sweep him into that magical, see-through land. And there, in a fortress filled with castaway children, a two-hundred-year-old riddle lies buried. The most important boy in Echoland will help Will solve it with a handful of other teens. For the fate of Echoland, and of the Sound realm, depends on the answer.

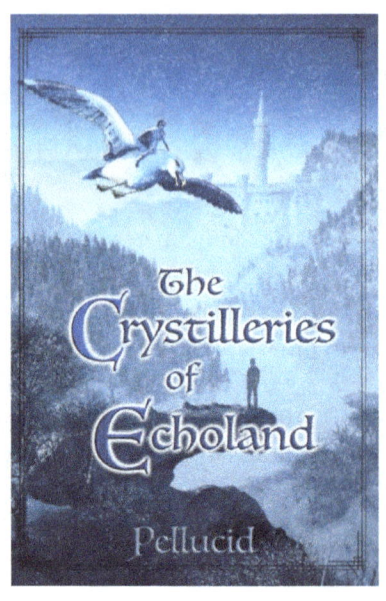

The Book of Esther, also known as the Megillah, is one of the five stories in the Writings section of the Old Testament. The story is well known to both Christians and Jews as the tale of the heroic Esther, who saves her people from annihilation by the evil Haman. The holiday of Purim is celebrated every year by the Jewish community with costumes, parades, and tri-cornered fruit-filled pastries called Hamentashen.

But before Esther, there was Vashti, the king's first wife. Her defiance of his order to debase herself for the amusement of his cronies led to her being banished from the kingdom. This paved the way for Esther to take her place, and Vashti was never heard from again.

This book takes the reader on a significant journey through the inspirational stories of the Old Testament. It offers a comprehensive and accurate collection of more than 200 stories of the people and prophets of the Old Testament. The reader will find his favorite stories from childhood, along with many less familiar but equally moving accounts of faith and devotion, presented in the comfortable and reverent style of the author. In addition to memorable stories, the author has included extensive footnotes and reference material for readers seeking an in-depth study of the scriptures of the Old Testament.

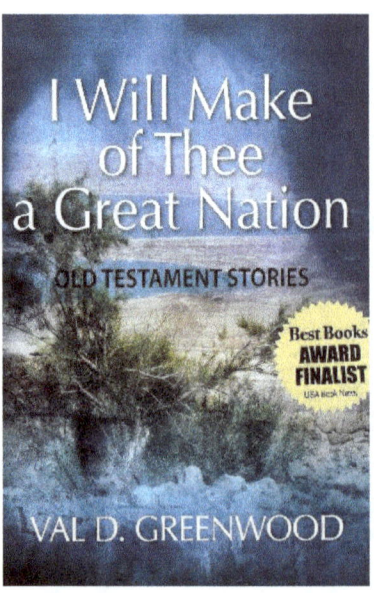